S0-EIH-197

▶ TRUTHS

about CHRISTIANS AND POLITICS

TEN TRUTHS ABOUT CHRISTIANS AND POLITICS

Cover and Interior Design: Roark Creative, www.roarkcreative.com

Published by Coral Ridge Ministries

Printed in the United States of America

CORAL RIDGE
MINISTRIES

Dr. D. James Kennedy, Founder

PROCLAIMING TRUTHS THAT
TRANSFORM THE WORLD

Post Office Box 1920
Fort Lauderdale, Florida 33302
1-800-988-7884
www.coralridge.org
letters@coralridge.org

CONTENTS

CONTENTS

10 TRUTHS

about CHRISTIANS AND POLITICS

CHRISTIANITY IS A REVOLUTIONARY RELIGION.
IT NOT ONLY CHANGES INDIVIDUALS;
IT CHANGES CULTURES.

INTRODUCTION

In the first century, it did not take long before the shift in the moral universe introduced by Christ and his followers had struck a nerve. An angry mob at Thessalonica called for the arrest of Christian missionaries Paul and Silas, charging that "These who have turned the world upside down have come here too" (Acts 17:6).

An early Christian, Tetramachus, stepped into the Roman gladiator arena around 400 A.D. in an attempt to end the Roman blood sport. He was cut down as he tried to pull the combatants apart, but his courageous and lonely example prompted Emperor Honorius to abolish the games.

Into the Arena

Christians today, however, are none too eager to follow Tetramachus into the arena. Billy Graham wrote many years ago that in the face of our culture's social problems, Christians are too often "afflicted with moral laryngitis."[1] He stated:

Christianity grew because its adherents were not silent . . . . They stormed against the evils of their day until the very foundations of decadent Rome began to crumble. Is the church doing that today?[2]

Billy Graham
(American Vision)

Graham asked that question in 1962. Three years later, one prominent pastor answered it with an unqualified "No."

Believing the Bible as I do, I would find it impossible to stop preaching the pure saving gospel of Jesus Christ, and begin doing anything else—including fighting communism or participating in civil rights reforms. . . . Preachers are not called to be politicians, but to be soul winners. . . . Nowhere are we commissioned to reform the externals. The gospel does not clean up the outside, but rather regenerates the inside.[3]

Jerry Falwell
(Jerry Falwell Ministries)

That was Jerry Falwell in 1965. By 1979, when he formed the Moral Majority with D. James Kennedy and other Christian leaders, he had come to a dramatically different understanding of the Christian's civic responsibilities.

Yet echoes of the 1965 voice of Jerry Falwell can still be heard today across the evangelical landscape. Authors Cal Thomas and Ed Dobson have charged that Christians in politics have precious little to show for their long trek through the political wilderness.

Bible teacher John MacArthur has published a broadside against Christian civic engagement and believes that the church should not be engaged in legislative battles.

There is, of course, reason for caution when it comes to Christian civic involvement. Church history is littered with tragic examples of what happens when the power of the state is used to impose obedience to the gospel. The Inquisitions are a stain on the church and demonstrate the danger of placing the power of cross and crown in the same hands.

That is not the biblical model, as this short booklet explains. Despite medieval abuses, we Christians have a powerful, positive example in our own nation of what happens when believers engage in the political process. The majority of America's founders were Christians who took their civic duties seriously. Their efforts laid the foundation for the freest and most prosperous nation in history.

Basic Truths About God and Government

Ten Truths About Christians and Politics presents basic truths about God and government, many of them well known to our nation's founders. Our aim, frankly, is to give you historical and biblical perspective that will arm you for action. After all, the need is enormous—the cause of defending the unborn alone could absorb the energies of a lifetime.

At the September 2007 memorial service for Dr. D. James Kennedy, Dr. James Dobson noted the passing in recent years of a number of Christian moral leaders, including Adrian Rogers, Jerry Falwell, Bill Bright, and D. James Kennedy. He asked who will fill the void left by these moral leaders:

Dr. James Dobson

Who will defend the unborn child; who will speak for them? Who will speak for those who are older and no longer productive? Who will plead for the Terri Schiavos of the world who can be starved to death legally for having the misfortune of being disabled? Who has the courage to speak up? Who is going to fight for the institution of marriage . . . and teach young people the dangers of heterosexual and homosexual promiscuity? Who will, in the next generation, be willing to take the heat when it is so much safer and comfortable to avoid controversy?[4]

Today, thankfully, we do not need to enter the gladiatorial arena like Tetramachus to stop the killing, but we do need the moral courage of men like Bright, Falwell, Kennedy, and Rogers if these and other evils in our culture are to be challenged.

We cannot wait for a new generation of leaders to rise up to lead us. Each of us must take responsibility for carrying out our own Christian civic duty in the arena of government and politics. Our prayer is that this booklet will help you understand more clearly some of the basic truths about Christians and politics so that you may, along with many others, enter the arena.

TRUTH 1

The Foundation of Government
and Politics Is Religion

"Strictly separate." When it comes to religion and politics, that is the rule announced by the courts and enforced by the American Civil Liberties Union over the past sixty years.

In 1947, the U.S. Supreme Court reversed a longstanding American legal tradition and declared that the U.S. Constitution has erected a "high and impregnable"[5] wall of separation between church and state. The ACLU then set out to apply that ruling in the decades to follow, sending threatening letters and going into court to force civic officials to remove Ten Commandments displays, crèche scenes, the Bible, and even prayer from public life.

U.S. Supreme Court building

But while the ACLU has been tireless in its efforts to purge the Christian religion from public life, the truth is, religion is the foundation on which nations are built. And although ACLU attorneys may shudder at the thought, the Christian religion provides the surest foundation for the moral, political, and social order of any nation.

The importance of religion in providing the necessary foundation for any social order has been noted by acclaimed historians Will and Ariel Durant, who acknowledged in 1968 that "there is no significant example in history before our time of a society successfully maintaining moral life without the aid of religion."[6]

Every government needs a moral code to justify and legitimize its rule, and every lasting moral system must rest on religion—which answers the ultimate questions about man and God. Without religion to breathe life and meaning into any legal-political system, the options are either anarchy or tyranny.

Christianity and Western Pre-Eminence

Some argue, as did the Durants, that in our time such a religious foundation is no longer necessary. But the truth is evident, even to elite social scientists in Communist China. The "pre-eminence" of Western cultures and nations is due to the influence of Christianity.

Former *Time* magazine reporter David Aikman tells in his book, *Jesus in Beijing*, how a Chinese researcher explained that he and his colleagues "studied everything we could from the historical, political, economic, and cultural perspective," to understand Western dominance. The researcher explained:

At first, we thought it was because you had more powerful guns than we had. Then we thought it was because you had the best political system. Next we focused on your economic system. But in the past twenty years, we have realized that the heart of your culture is your religion: Christianity. That is why the West has been so powerful. The Christian moral foundation of social and cultural life was what made possible the emergence of capitalism and then the successful transition to democratic politics. We don't have any doubt about this.[7]

What these Chinese scholars found to be true for the West was recognized very clearly by our nation's founders. President John Adams, signer of both the Declaration of Independence and the U.S. Constitution, put it this way:

We have no government armed with power capable of contending with human passions unbridled by morality and religion. Avarice, ambition, revenge, or gallantry would break the strongest cords of our Constitution as a whale goes through a net. Our Constitution was made only for a moral and religious people. It is wholly inadequate to the government of any other.[8]

John Adams (American Vision)

Despite the record of history, the ACLU and its friends are adamant in their insistence that America is a secular nation. What Catholic priest and writer Richard John Neuhaus has called the "naked public square," has become the ruling orthodoxy for contemporary American political thought.

Government by Guillotine

It is a modern innovation and one, if you consult the French Revolution, that doesn't work out so well. The short-lived French Revolution (1789-1799) was so thoroughgoing in its rejection of Christianity that it even established a new calendar without Sundays. During its infamous Reign of Terror, the streets of Paris flowed with blood and tens of thousands of people were guillotined.[9]

As Ernest Renan, a nineteenth century French agnostic, stated:

If Rationalism wishes to govern the world without regard to the religious needs of the soul, the experience of the French Revolution is there to teach us the consequences of such a blunder.[10]

And since Renan, Nazi, fascist, and communist regimes, all of which rejected God and religious belief, have shown, again, that once religion is removed, a door opens into the abyss. The death toll from Lenin, Stalin, Mao, and their fellow communist henchmen is nearly 100 million people, according to *The Black Book of Communism*.[11] Here in America, the court-ordered departure from America's Christian moral framework has already resulted in the death of more than 48 million people—all of them unborn.[12]

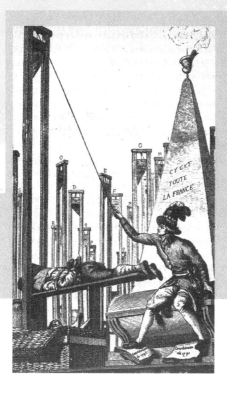

The French Revolution introduced a "reign of terror."
(American Vision)

State-Mandated Secularism

Despite this sobering testimony from history, American law and politics have over the past decades moved toward the view, as stated by Barry Lynn, executive director of Americans United for Separation of Church and State, that "[i]n the United States, secularism is mandated for the government."[13] "Mandated" is an aptly chosen word since "we, the people," have not had any say in the matter. "Many Americans," as Richard John Neuhaus writes, "feel that they were not consulted by whoever decided that this is a secular society. And they resent that; they resent it very much."[14]

State-mandated secularism, imposed by the courts and enforced by the ACLU and its allies, is a leading flashpoint in America's

Barry Lynn, left, seated next to Dr. D. James Kennedy at a U.S. House of Representatives committee hearing in 2002.
(Mattox Photography)

ongoing culture war between competing Christian and secular moral visions for the nation. One side looks to the Christian foundations of this country; the other provides no moral basis for American politics and government at all. It's a pity that the quarrel exists at all since, when you look at the record, not only is religion needed to found and sustain a state but, as we will see in the following chapter, Christianity makes the best foundation by far.

TRUTH 2

Christianity Makes the Best
Foundation for Law and Politics

Christianity brought a moral overhaul to the ancient world that is most evident in the treatment before and after Christ of the "least of these," little children. What we take for granted about cherishing the young was not always so.

In 1 B.C. a Roman traveler to Alexandria, Egypt, sent a warm note home to his wife. It was a tender letter, with one chilling exception:

> I send you my warmest greetings. I want you to know that we are still in Alexandria. And please don't worry if all the others come home, but I remain in Alexandria. I beg you and entreat you to take care of the child and, if I receive my pay soon, I will send it up to you. If you have the baby before I return, if it is a boy, let it live; if it is a girl, expose it. You sent a message with Aphrodisias, "Don't forget me." How can I forget you? I beg you, then, not to worry.[15]

This blunt and matter of fact direction to discard a baby girl offers stark and troubling insight into the moral character of the ancient Roman world, where infanticide was common. Nineteenth century Irish historian W.E.H. Lecky called infanticide "one of the deepest stains of the ancient civilization."[16] It was so much a part of Roman culture that the myth of the founding of Rome recounts the abandonment of two infants, Romulus and Remus. Thrown into the Tiber River in the eighth century B.C., they were said to have survived by being nursed by wolves.[17]

Opposition to Infanticide

"Not only was the exposure of infants a very common practice, it was justified by law and advocated by philosophers," including both Plato and Aristotle.[18] The Roman tradition of *paterfamilias* gave the father total authority to decide the fate of his children— including whether a newborn was to be exposed to die outside the city walls, or allowed to live.[19]

Early Christians followed the example of Jesus, who loved and blessed the children, as recorded in Matthew 19:14. They firmly opposed abortion and infanticide. Two early church documents that were widely read, the *Didache* and the *Epistle of Barnabas*, both prohibited infanticide.[20] Eventually, these Christian views became Roman law. Emperor Valentinian, who had been lobbied by Bishop Basil of Caesarea, outlawed infanticide in 374 A.D.[21] and in 529, Emperor Justinian emancipated all "exposed" children who had been forced into slavery.[22]

Slavery was widespread in the ancient world, but it was not opposed by church fathers with the same firmness as infanticide. Still, Paul made it clear that in Christ, "there is neither slave nor free . . . for you are all one in Christ Jesus" (Galatians 3:28). By the fourth century, legal reforms to benefit slaves were adopted under the first Christian emperor, Constantine.[23]

Jesus Christ loved and blessed little children.

As Christianity spread throughout the ancient world, its influence was felt in other areas of the law. Constantine, for example, also ended the practice of branding criminals on the forehead because, he said, "The human countenance, formed after the image of heavenly beauty, should not be defaced."[24]

In the sixth century, Emperor Justinian reorganized the Roman legal code and essentially "enacted orthodox Christianity into law," according to historian Will Durant.[25] Charles Diehl, author of a history of the Byzantine Empire, states that Justinian's Code "introduced into law a regard, hitherto unknown, for social justice, public morality, and humanity."[26]

Rule of Law

The Roman Caesars, unfettered by legal or moral restrictions, had been prone to mercilessly dispatching their victims to death. Historian Alvin Schmidt reports that Tiberius enjoyed seeing his torture victims thrown into the sea, and a suspicious Caligula had his entire palace staff killed.[27] Christianity, however, brought both a new ethic and new ideas about the limits of civil authority. Ambrose, the fourth century bishop of Milan, rebuked Emperor Theodosius I, telling him that "No one, not even the emperor, is above the law."[28] That challenge to the sovereignty of the Caesars, who required worship from their subjects and often threw them to the lions for refusing to do so, was a new thought for the ancient world.

King Alfred the Great
(American Vision)

It was a Christian idea that the king, like his subjects, was subject to the law. As Christianity took root, so did this revolutionary idea, and slowly it worked its way into Western law. As the first British monarch to rule over all of England, King Alfred the Great (849-899) placed English law on an explicitly biblical foundation, drawing from "the Ten Commandments, the Laws of Moses, the Golden rule of Christ, and other

Bishop Ambrose told Roman Emperor Theodosius I that "No one, not even the emperor, is above the law."

(American Vision)

biblical principles."[29] According to one commentator, King Alfred's published laws "were a creative effort of government unique in Europe and marked the beginning of a great age for England."[30] As the Bible was applied to civic law, "the Christian church effected nothing short of a revolution in the forms of Western politics."[31] King Alfred also saw the connection between an educated populace and effective government and he promoted general education and insisted that his nobles read and learn Christian history. His view of government, he wrote, was that:

Local government ought to be synonymous with local Christian virtue, otherwise it becomes local tyranny, local corruption and local iniquity.[32]

The idea that even the king was subject to the rule of law was tested 300 years later by the tyrannical rule of King John. But in 1215, the English barons, with the help of the Archbishop of

Canterbury, Stephen Langton, and other ecclesiastical leaders, forced the king to submit himself to a written charter. The Magna Carta placed specific limitations on the king's rule and, according to an American Bar Foundation publication, it provided "the foundation on which has come to rest the entire structure of Anglo-American constitutional liberties."[33] This landmark document, which clearly rested on the Holy Scriptures, later served as the cornerstone for the American colonists' claim that King George III had violated their rights as British subjects.

"The Bible," as Dr. D. James Kennedy has written, "laid the foundations and principles upon which the Magna Carta was framed."[34] But can the Bible serve as a political handbook? The next chapter answers that question.

King John
(American Vision)

TRUTH 3

The Bible Gives Guidance for Governments and Citizens

The Bible is very much a political handbook. After all, its central figure is the "King of Kings and Lord of Lords" and many of its lesser characters—Moses, Joshua, Samson, Deborah, David, Solomon, and Daniel—were all political leaders. Two Old Testament books are called "Kings."

The Bible gives us both the Mosaic legal code—a detailed set of civil laws designed for ancient Israel, but with clear applications for modern states—as well as a set of first principles to guide our thinking about civil government.

Lord of All—Including Politics

The first such principle is that God is sovereign—even over politics. The psalmist cries out that "The Lord has established His throne in heaven, and His kingdom rules over all" (Psalm 103:19). "To deny that this area [politics] of decision-making is to be affected by religion is to deny the lordship of Jesus Christ over a particular area of life,"[35] writes historian Gary DeMar, president of American Vision.

Gary DeMar
(American Vision)

God also determines who's up and who's down. Civil rulers, ultimately, are "elected" by God: "But God is the Judge: He puts down one, and exalts

Moses and the Ten Commandments
(Library of Congress)

another" (Psalm 75:7). Pharaoh held sway over Egypt and the children of Israel—but only because God placed him there for a reason. "But indeed for this purpose," God told Pharaoh through Moses, "I have raised you up, that I may show My power in you, and that My name may be declared in all the earth" (Exodus 9:16).

A primary purpose of civil government is to provide order and justice to restrain the wicked acts of men so that citizens may be free to seek God. Paul told Greek thinkers that God "made from one blood every nation of men to dwell on all the face of the earth, and has determined their preappointed times and the boundaries of their dwellings, so that they should seek the Lord" (Acts 17:26-27). Toward that end, Christians are told to pray "for kings and all who are in authority, that we may lead a quiet and peaceable life in all godliness and reverence" (1 Timothy 2:1-3).

Separation of Church and State in the Bible

The Bible also teaches—and this may surprise you—the separation of church and state. Now this doesn't mean a wall should quarantine Christians from the civic life of the nation. Rather, this is a biblically based distinction which allots to church and state separate duties under God's sovereign reign. The ancient Jewish king Uzziah discovered that distinction, to his great regret, when he tried to usurp the role of the priests.

Uzziah had become proud, the Scripture states, and "transgressed against the Lord his God by entering the temple of the Lord to burn incense on the altar of incense" (2 Chronicles 26:16). He was king, but had no authority to act as priest. Some 80 priests, led by Azariah, quickly confronted Uzziah, mustering courage and telling their king in no uncertain terms to "Get out of the sanctuary, for you have trespassed!" (2 Chronicles 26:18). Uzziah's angry reply did not escape God's judgment. Leprosy appeared on his forehead and he was hustled from the sanctuary by the priests.

Uzziah spent his remaining years in isolation; his kingdom was given to his son, and he never entered the temple again. This is clear evidence for how seriously God takes the division of labor he has ordained between church and state.

Jesus acknowledged the separation of church and state when a few of his adversaries tried to corner him by asking if it was lawful for an observant Jew to pay taxes to Caesar. Christ saw their true agenda and answered them by pointing to a Roman coin which bore the image of Caesar. "Render to Caesar the things that are Caesar's," he told his questioners, "and to God the things that are God's" (Mark 12:17).

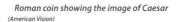

Along with showing the image of Caesar, the coin in Christ's hand bore an inscription that was "virtu-

Roman coin showing the image of Caesar
(American Vision)

Apostle Paul
(American Vision)

ally an ascription of deity to the reigning emperor...."[36] The blasphemous Roman requirement to worship Caesar, which was indicated on the coin, was a "thing" owed to God, not to man.[37] Christians, then, are obligated to obey the state when it acts within the limits of the "things that are Caesar's." But when Caesar invades the sanctuary and exceeds his authority, Christians have a duty to resist.

Duty to Obey and to Disobey

Paul instructed Christians in Rome to "be subject to the governing authorities" (Romans 13:1) and to pay their taxes. Those who disobey the state, he wrote, resist "the ordinance of God, and those who resist will bring judgment on themselves" (Romans 13:2).

However, the Bible also demonstrates that unrighteous decrees are not to be obeyed. The Hebrew midwives feared God more than the king of Egypt and disobeyed his cruel command to kill newborn Hebrew boys. God blessed them as a result: "And so it was, because the midwives feared God, that He provided households for them" (Exodus 1:21).

Shortly after the resurrection and ascension of Jesus, Jewish authorities grew troubled at the growth of His followers and strictly instructed Peter and the other apostles against teaching about Christ. The apostles refused, telling the high priest, "We ought to obey God rather than men" (Acts 5:29).

Along with the duty to disobey unrighteous commands, the Bible indicates that God's people have a duty to confront political authorities who stray from God's moral standard. The Old Testament often recounts how the prophets confronted the Jewish monarchs with God's verdict upon their unrighteous behavior. The prophet Samuel announced God's judgment on King Saul for his disregard of God's word to him (1 Samuel 15:22-23). Elijah challenged wicked King Ahab over his Baal worship and was called the "troubler of Israel" for his effort (1 Kings 18:17). Nathan

The prophet Nathan confronts King David.
(American Vision)

confronted David for his sin with Bathsheba and the murder of her husband, Uriah (2 Samuel 12).

Besides confronting evil and refusing to go along with it, there is another role outlined for the saints in both the Old and New Testament—to be "salt and light." God, through Jeremiah, told the Jewish exiles in Babylon to "seek the peace of the city where I have caused you to be carried away captive, and pray to the Lord

Christ's followers are to bring the flavor of God's grace and the healing and preserving power of His Word into every area of life—

including the world of politics.

for it; for in its peace you will have peace" (Jeremiah 29:7). The exiles were not to withdraw from their ungodly environment into a cultural enclave, but rather to seek its peace or *shalom*—a Hebrew term also translated as "welfare."

Sodium Saints

Jesus calls his people to be like salt in their influence on the world around them (Matthew 5:13). Just as salt was used in first century Israel to flavor and preserve food or to cleanse wounds, Christ's followers are to bring the flavor of God's grace and the healing and preserving power of His Word into every area of life—including the world of politics.

Christians in America at the time of our founding took that role—and the Bible's relevance for political questions—as a given, and they built a land that is unique among nations. The next chapter shows, however, what happens when governments try to keep God and His laws out of the equation.

TRUTH 4

Without God, Government
Is a Fearful Master

Bursting with confidence, a small group composed mostly of Unitarian clergymen and academics issued their "Humanist Manifesto" in 1933. Advances in science and economics, they announced, had made it possible to reject God and traditional religions in favor of a new "religious humanism."

"Man is at last becoming aware," they burbled, "that he alone is responsible for the realization of the world of his dreams, that he has within himself the power for its achievement."[38]

Humanism in Practice

That same year, Soviet dictator Joseph Stalin approved the genocide of seven million Ukrainians, and Adolf Hitler seized power in Germany. While American humanists enthused about "a free and universal society in which people voluntarily and intelligently cooperate for the common good," their ideological cousins in the Kremlin were imposing policies that wiped out almost 25 percent of the Ukraine population, including some three million children.[39]

Joseph Stalin
(American Vision)

In 1933, while these American humanists were joining in a chorus of praise to man's

Man starved by Soviet-engineered famine in Ukraine, 1932-33.
(ITAR-TASS/ Vladimir Sindeyev)

potential to realize his dreams without the help of God, Europe's two largest nations, led by Stalin and Hitler, were "firmly in the grip of totalitarian regimes which preached and practiced, and indeed embodied, moral relativism, with all its horrifying potentialities."[40] While the American humanists were heralding a social vision that banished God, across the Atlantic that vision was being put into practice.

Both Stalin, who had become an atheist after reading Darwin, and Hitler, who tried to speed up evolution by eliminating "inferior" humans, ruled without moral restraint. They lived out what Lenin called "the scientific concept of dictatorship." By that he meant "power without limit, resting directly upon force, restrained by no laws, absolutely unrestricted by rules."[41]

Don't Stop Clapping

Under their rule, "Fear by night, and a feverish effort by day to pretend enthusiasm for a system of lies, was the permanent condition," according to historian Robert Conquest.[42] Soviet cruelty included a sentence of ten years prison time to a man who was first to stop clapping for Comrade Stalin after he spoke.[43] An unfortunate tailor received a sentence of ten years because when he laid aside his needle, he "stuck it into a newspaper on the wall so it wouldn't get lost and happened to stick it in the eye of a portrait of Kaganovich [a member of the Soviet Politburo]."[44]

Hitler, who made it his business to commandeer the church to his purposes, was pitiless toward all of so-called inferior race. "Our strength is in our quickness and our brutality," he told SS troops just before the invasion of Poland in August 1939. According to Hitler:

> **Genghis Khan had millions of women and children killed by his own will and with a gay heart. History sees in him only a great state builder. Thus, for the time being, I have sent to the East only my "Death's Head Units" with orders to kill without pity or mercy all men, women, and children of Polish race or lineage.**[45]

By speaking of his belief in "God," Hitler would mobilize the German people with his rhetoric. His toxic racial ideas were built on Darwinian blind chance, and although publicly pious, he rejected the Creator God of Scripture. He consistently tried to use the church for Nazi ends, telling two bishops of the South German Evangelical Church that "Christianity will disappear from Germany just as it has in Russia."[46]

Neither Hitler nor Stalin ever signed the Humanist Manifesto, but their beliefs were the same as several of its key planks, including the following:

1) **there is no Creator**
2) **man evolved and is part of nature with no special status as one made in the image of God**
3) **there are no moral absolutes**[47]

Both Hitler and Stalin would have smiled in approval of these statements. Yet these two failed rulers of failed states clearly show what happens when men and nations remove God from politics. The death toll from Hitler's mad tyranny was some 13 million people.[48] Russian historian Dmitri Volkogonov has put the loss of life during Stalin's repressive regime at 21.5 million.[49] As Ivan

> ## "Christianity will disappear from Germany just as it has in Russia."
>
> **Adolf Hitler**
> (American Vision)

Karamazov, the atheist character in Dostoevsky's nineteenth century novel, *The Brother Karamazov*, famously said, "[E]verything is permitted . . . since there is no infinite God, there's no such thing as virtue either and there's no need for it at all."[50]

America's Founders Knew Better

Despite the recent lessons of Russia and Germany, many in America want to push ahead with the humanist agenda and erect a permanent partition between God and government. America's Founders knew better. They acknowledged the existence of God as Creator, affirmed moral absolutes ("laws of nature and of nature's God") in the Declaration of Independence, and gave birth to the most free and prosperous nation in history.

The Founders took seriously the Bible's claim that man is sinful, and they framed a government with checks against human depravity. James Madison explained it this way:

But what is government itself, but the greatest of all reflections on human nature? If men were angels, no government would be necessary. If angels were to govern men, neither external nor internal controls on government would be necessary. In framing a government which is to be administered by men over men, the great difficulty lies in this: you must first enable the government to control the governed; and in the next place oblige it to control itself. A dependence on the people is, no doubt, the primary control on the government; but experience has taught mankind the necessity of auxiliary precautions.[51]

James Madison
(American Vision)

Guided in their "reflections on human nature" by the testimony of Scripture and history, the Founders were supremely skeptical of any claims for human goodness. They crafted a government filled with safeguards against human evil. They recognized then, as we must now, that the Bible offers political wisdom and guidance. They well understood, as the next chapter shows, what the Bible says about these topics.

TRUTH 5

America Was Built by Biblically Literate Citizens

He is the most influential Founder you've never heard of—and he was typical of his generation. Dr. Benjamin Rush (1745-1813) was, at his death, one of the three most well-known and well-regarded Founding Fathers, along with George Washington and Benjamin Franklin.[52] Today, however, you will not find him in high school American history textbooks.

Rush believed that "patriotism is both a moral and a religious duty."[53] He was a signer of the Declaration of Independence and urged Thomas Paine to publish *Common Sense*, providing him with the title. He served in the Continental Congress and was physician general of the Continental Army.

At his death, Thomas Jefferson wrote, ". . . a better man than Rush could not have left us, more benevolent, more learned, of finer genius, or more honest."[54] Author John Sanderson wrote of Rush in 1823:

Benjamin Rush
(American Vision)

In all the periods of his life, he was remarkable for his attention to religious duties and his reverence for the Holy Scriptures. He urges, in all his writings, the excellency of the Christian faith and its happy influence upon the social habits of the country.[55]

Seminary-Trained Declaration Signers

Rush, who helped launch the American Sunday School movement and the Bible Society of Philadelphia, was not alone among America's founders in his religious convictions. Historian David Barton reports that almost half of the signers of the Declaration (24 out of 56) held what today would be considered seminary or Bible school degrees.[56]

Rush's life shows in microcosm what is sometimes denied and often overlooked: America began as an enterprise of Christian religious liberty and is the product of deeply committed and biblically literate Christian citizens. Alexis de Tocqueville, a Frenchman who toured our nation in the early 1830s, wrote in *Democracy in America*, "It must never be forgotten that religion gave birth to Anglo-American society."[57]

Alexis de Tocqueville
(American Vision)

Daniel Webster, a nineteenth century statesman who served as a Congressman, a Senator from Massachusetts, and as U.S. Secretary of State, looked back at America's origins in an 1820 speech commemorating the 200th anniversary of the Pilgrims' arrival:

> Our fathers were brought hither by their high veneration for the Christian religion. They journeyed in its hope. They sought to incorporate its principles with the elements of their society, and to diffuse its influence through all their institutions, civil, political, or literary.[58]

Sermons: More Powerful Than TV

The men who drafted our nation's founding documents and fought the American War for Independence were products of a 150-year-old colonial culture that was self-consciously Christian.

Nowhere was this more evident than in New England, where the primary vehicle for the inculcation of values—spiritual, moral, and political—was the Sunday sermon. In an age without iPods, cable television, news-talk radio, or the Internet, there was precious little to compete with sermons, which were delivered twice on Sunday and sometimes once during the week. According to historian Harry Stout, New England sermons were "so powerful in shaping cultural values, meanings, and a sense of corporate purpose that even television pales in comparison."[59]

The average weekly churchgoer, he writes, heard close to 7,000 sermons in a lifetime, representing about "fifteen thousand hours of concentrated listening."[60] These sermons addressed nearly every question and area of life—including politics.

Beginning in 1634, election-day sermons—which focused on civic duty and the mission of New England—were preached at the outset of the civil year to a joint assembly of ministers and civil magistrates. These annual sermons, which were printed and distributed, served to direct the public mind to the demands of God's Word and to remind leaders of New England's unique mission—its "errand into the wilderness."

← **WITH AN OPEN GENEVA BIBLE,** the Pilgrims pray as they embark for the New World on July 22, 1620.

(Architect of the U.S. Capitol)

In a 1677 election-day sermon, Puritan minister Increase Mather told his audience:

It was love to God and to Jesus Christ which brought our fathers into this wilderness. . . . There never was a generation that did so perfectly shake off the dust of Babylon, both as to ecclesiastical and civil constitution, as the first generation of Christians that came into this land for the gospel's sake.[61]

John Calvin: "Father of America"

The original spark for that errand across the Atlantic came from the Reformation and the reformer John Calvin (1509-1564). The influence of Calvin was so pronounced that nineteenth century historian George Bancroft called him "the father of America."[62] Colonial leaders embraced Calvin's ideas about resistance to tyranny and the Presbyterian system of church government, which he articulated from Scripture and which offered colonists a laboratory for self-government.

Reformation ideas were propagated through the Geneva Bible, which was first published in 1560 and was widely used by the Pilgrims and Puritans. Just as with some of the study Bibles of today, it had marginal commentaries that were the work of Reformation scholars who had been driven from England by

Bloody Mary and King James I.[63] Those side-bar notes so provoked King James' ire that he commissioned his own official version, the King James Bible, which duly had all "seditious" commentary, as he called it, removed.

John Calvin
(H.H. Meeter Center for Calvin Studies, Calvin College)

Falling back to an earlier era, James embraced the Greco-Roman theory of the "divine right of kings," which held that the monarch was accountable only to God for his actions. It also made the claim that total obedience was due the king by his subjects on all matters, both civil and ecclesiastical.

This doctrine would have served as an effective prop to James' rule, but it was severely undermined by the Geneva Bible, which proved to be so popular with his subjects that it went through 144 editions between 1560 and 1644.[64] One passage that James no doubt would have found offensive was the note on Exodus 1:9, stating that the Hebrew midwives acted properly in disregarding the command of Egypt's king to kill newborn male Hebrew babies.

Widely distributed and uncompromising in its application of Scripture to the civic arena, the Geneva Bible, as Dr. Marshall Foster, founder and president of the Mayflower Institute, writes, "began the unstoppable march to liberty in England, Scotland, and America."[65]

TRUTH 6

All Governments Legislate Morality

"You can't legislate morality." Everyone knows that. Even Jesse Ventura, the former professional wrestler and one-term Minnesota governor has body-slammed the idea that legislators can and should pass laws on moral matters. "[T]he old saw, 'You can't legislate morality,' still rings true," he writes. "It's been tried. It doesn't work."[66]

This widely used catch phrase is a popular idea with durable roots in recent American history. John F. Kennedy stood before an audience of Baptist ministers in 1960 to assure them—and the nation—that, if elected president, his personal religious faith would not interfere with how he performed his duties. Twenty-four years later, then governor of New York, Mario Cuomo, gave a speech at Notre Dame to explain why he, though personally pro-life, would not impose his morality on the voters of New York.

John F. Kennedy
(American Vision)

Opposition to the use of law to enact one's personal moral beliefs goes back even further. President James Buchanan was personally opposed to the institution of slavery, but he took no action to end it. Buchanan, who served as president from 1857 to 1861, was more concerned about roads and revenue than human bondage. He viewed abolitionists as divisive, and

James Buchanan
(Library of Congress)

thought, according to biographer Philip S. Klein, that "questions of morality could not be settled by political action."[67]

But would anyone defend slavery or use that argument to do so today? Hardly. The nation finally settled the matter of slavery—first by war and then by the thirteenth amendment to the U.S. Constitution, which imposed an anti-slavery morality on the entire nation. Maybe Jesse and his friends are incorrect. Maybe we can, and should, legislate morality.

Slaves on a southern plantation
(American Vision)

Actually we do—every day. Laws against theft, murder, drug use, and prostitution, to list just a few, all impose morality on the public. All law, like it or not, arises from a view of morality and is rooted in religious values. This is both unavoidable and indispensable. "It is religion and morality alone which can establish the principles upon which freedom can securely stand," said John Adams, who signed the Declaration of Independence and later served as America's second president.[68]

Double Standard on Legislating Morals

Interestingly, those who seek to impose morality on the nation are sometimes celebrated, not censured. The Rev. Martin Luther King, Jr. effectively imposed his moral values on Lester Maddox and George Wallace, segregationist governors of Georgia and Alabama. Now he is rightly praised for his moral leadership. And when the National Conference of Catholic Bishops said in 1983 that the use of nuclear weapons could never be morally justified,[69] Governor Cuomo praised them for their "courage and moral judgment."[70] As the late Henry Hyde pointed out, "The clergy were revered when they marched at Selma, joined antiwar sit-ins and helped boycott lettuce—they are reviled when they speak out against abortion."[71]

Henry Hyde
(Handout Photo)

He's right. No one objects when groups like the Religious Coalition for Reproductive Choice lobby and litigate on behalf of the right to puncture the skull and suction the brains out of a partially delivered baby. But as Hyde learned firsthand, Christians who seek to protect the unborn are accused of trying to impose their religion on the nation.

After Hyde, a U.S. Representative from 1975-2007, won passage in 1976 of an amendment to prohibit the use of federal funds for abortion, the American Civil Liberties Union and Planned Parenthood went to court to stop its enforcement. They argued that Hyde's law was religiously based and therefore "used the fist of government to smash the wall of separation between church and state. . . ."[72] To prove their argument, they demanded and won the right to inspect his mail for evidence of religious sentiment and hired a private eye who tailed Hyde into St. Thomas More Cathedral in Arlington, Virginia, where he attended a mass to pray for the unborn.

Fortunately, the ACLU/Planned Parenthood lawsuit failed in 1980, when the U.S. Supreme Court, by a narrow 5-4 margin, upheld the Hyde amendment. Hyde, however, said, "The anger I felt when they tried to disenfranchise me because of my religion has stayed with me. These are dangerous people who make dangerous arguments."[73]

Law Can Lead to Changed Attitudes

One of those arguments—the claim, made by Gov. Ventura, that legislating morality doesn't work—is just not true. The law won't change someone's heart, but it will restrain behavior, and it can lead to changed attitudes. "It may be true that you cannot legislate morality," Martin Luther King, Jr. said in 1965, "but behavior can be regulated. It may be true that the law cannot make a man love me, but it can restrain him from lynching me, and I think that is pretty important also."[74]

And laws do impact public opinion. Attitudes about slavery have turned around dramatically since 1861, when the nation went to war to settle the question. "Legislating against slavery helped change attitudes because the majority of people have always believed that whatever is illegal must be immoral," say Dr. Norman Geisler and Frank Turek, authors of *Legislating Morality*.[75]

The Real Question: Whose Morality?

The real question is not *whether* morality should be legislated, but *whose* morality will be enacted into law. Geisler and Turek charge that the morality of secular humanism has been progressively imposed on the nation by the courts since the 1960s. In 1963 the U.S. Supreme Court removed Bible reading from the nation's schools. In the 1970s it legalized abortion. In the 1990s, Ten Commandments displays were removed from public venues and prayer was prohibited at graduations and high school football games. It should not have come as a surprise when the Court struck down the remaining sodomy laws in 2003. It was during this time, between 1960 and the early 1990s, that illegitimacy soared—up 450 percent; violent crime escalated—up 370 percent; teenage suicide increased dramatically—up 210 percent; and divorce increased by nearly 130 percent.[76]

Martin
Luther King, Jr.
(National Archives and
Records Administration)

Humanism, which holds that man is the measure of all things, is a social philosophy that simply does not work. It empties the public square of any divine promise or retribution. The United States is clearly reaping the social chaos that follows from the failure to "legislate morality."

The mantra, "You can't legislate morality!" is primarily a tool used to intimidate Christians and keep them from bringing salt and light to the realm of politics. Christians who work to make biblical morality the basis for our laws are not violating the Constitution—they are exercising the very liberty it guarantees. It is time we Christians take full advantage of that freedom. The next chapter shows, however, that when we do, we must make a choice as to *how* we will exercise our influence.

TRUTH 7

Retreat or Rule:
Neither Is an Option

When it comes to civic engagement, Christians face two temptations. One is to retreat into the safe confines of our stained-glass ghettos, where we can focus on worship, prayer, and Bible study. The other, widely practiced in past centuries, is to become the church militant and seek to establish Christ's kingdom by force—to use the sword of the state to extend God's rule into human hearts.

But neither "escape religion" nor "power religion," to use American Vision president Gary DeMar's terms, meets the standard set out in God's Word.[77] It is just as wrong to privatize one's faith as it is to politicize it. Both have been tried. Both miss the mark.

From Faith to Force

Emperor Constantine
(American Vision)

The early church endured nearly 300 years of bloody persecution until 313 A.D., when Roman emperor Constantine legalized Christianity. No more were Christians to be arrested, tortured, and executed. Suddenly, Christianity was legal and had the favor of friends in high places. However, that favor came at a cost. "The church, after Constantine, adopted Roman methods of rule and began to see the state as an ally," writes Benjamin Hart, author of *Faith and Freedom: The Christian Roots of American Liberty*. "Instead of proselytizing to make converts, it began an attempt to force belief."[78] Unfortunately, this is the template for church-state relations that was largely followed until the Pilgrims came ashore in 1620.

When Emperor Theodosius made Christianity the official religion in 380 A.D., he required all civic officials to adopt the Christian faith. A short five years later, a bishop from Spain became the first victim of the new state religion when he was tortured and decapitated for straying into Gnosticism.[79]

Even Augustine, a hero to many in the church, was willing, after much struggle, to use the power of the state to punish heretics. Charles Colson, author of *Kingdoms in Conflict*, writes that the Byzantine Empire functioned as a theocracy, with "the church serving as its department of spiritual affairs."[80] Charlemagne, whose empire contained much of what is now Western Europe, combined the church and state in 800 A.D. Only 44 years later, Charles the Bald inaugurated the Inquisitions to insure faithfulness to church teaching.[81]

The Pilgrims arrive at Plymouth Rock in 1620.
(American Vision)

Persecution of Christians at Rome
(American Vision)

Martin Luther: No to Church-State Marriage

This marriage of church and state, which had led to such horrible abuses, was rejected by Martin Luther and other leaders of the Reformation. Luther stated the principle in his usual forthright manner:

> The temporal lords want to rule the church, and, conversely, the theologians want to play the lord in the town hall. Under the papacy, mixing the two was considered ruling well, and it is still so considered. But in reality this is ruling very badly. . . .[82]

Charles Colson
(Zondervan Publishing)

Nevertheless, it was not until Reformation principles, grounded in Scripture, took root and blossomed in America that the pattern of uneasy alliance between church and state came to an end. "By refusing to assign redemptive powers to the state or to allow coercive power to the church," writes Colson, "the American experiment separated these two institutions for the first time since Constantine."[83]

Problems With Pietism

The opposite extreme, *pietism,* avoids all political involvement and seeks to engage exclusively in the pursuit of personal spiritual growth and the disciplines of prayer, Bible study, worship, and evangelism. This was the option initially chosen by Jerry Falwell who, as noted in the Introduction, was apolitical early in his ministry. While he later reversed himself, Falwell believed in 1965 that "preachers are not called to be politicians, but to be soul winners.... Nowhere are we commissioned to reform the externals. The gospel does not clean up the outside, but rather regenerates the inside."[84]

Pietism can be traced back to Jacob Spener, a church leader in the seventeenth century. He reacted against the cold religious formalism he saw in the German Lutheran church of his day by focusing on the disciplines of personal spirituality. But Spener's "healthy protest" soon decayed, according to Francis Schaeffer, into an outlook that sharply divided the "spiritual" from the "material" world. "The totality of human existence was not afforded a proper place," wrote Schaeffer. "In particular, it neglected the intellectual dimension of Christianity."[85]

D. James Kennedy has suggested that true Christianity is, in its effect, like a hurricane—with a warm, calm center and powerful swirling winds just beyond its core. Pietism, he said, is that warm center without the swirling winds that make a cultural impact. The result is cultural irrelevance and inattention to broader cultural shifts.[86] Francis Schaeffer also points out that a pietistic orientation

caused Christians to be slow to understand the modern shift from a Reformation-based to a humanist culture.[87]

Law professor Harold Berman shares the analysis of both Drs. Schaeffer and Kennedy, stating that, "… though religion is flourishing in America, it is increasingly a 'privatized' religion, with little in it that can overcome the forces of strife and disorder in society."[88]

Lesson From Nazi Germany

The dangers posed by pietism are illustrated by events in the 1930s in Nazi Germany. When Hitler moved quickly, after seizing power, to bend the church to his purposes, a small group of evangelicals resisted, but most evangelicals had little stomach for the fight. Under the influence of pietism, they "wanted to retreat into the sacristy."[89] Historian J.S. Conway writes:

> **Both their sense of loyalty to established power and their theological leanings, strongly influenced by the Pietistic tradition, inclined them towards a purely "spiritual" ministry, concerned only with individualistic salvation and ethics, and a readiness to obey the government's orders under all circumstances.**[90]

German evangelicals were largely silent on Nazi policy toward Jews, Gypsies, and other "undesirables." Some evangelicals, led by Martin Niemoller and Dietrich Bonhoeffer, mounted resistance, but there were too few willing to join them to stem the tide of evil that engulfed Germany and swept the civilized world into its vortex.

God's Mandate: "Have Dominion"

Pietism not only leads to cultural irrelevance, it is also a rejection of God's command to our first parents to "Be fruitful and multiply; fill the earth and subdue it; have dominion over the fish of the sea, over the birds of the air, and over every living thing that moves on the earth" (Genesis 1:28).

This *Cultural Mandate* from God does not divide the spiritual from the material. Instead, as Dr. Kennedy points out, "Man is to have dominion over all of the earth; he is to take all of the potentialities and possibilities of every phase of this world, and he is to culture it, improve it, and offer it all to God."[91]

No area of life, including government and politics, is exempt from God's command to "fill the earth and subdue it." Political questions are not beyond the scope of God's rule. They are addressed in Scripture, and Christians are called to exercise proper dominion in this arena just as much as in any other area of life—not that it will be easy. As we will see in the next chapter, John Knox found himself an unwelcome guest in the court of Mary, Queen of Scots. Yet this did not stop him from speaking biblical truth to her, even in the face of the temporal power that she held.

TRUTH 8

Christians Have the Duty to Speak Truth to Power

John Knox died in his own bed. Things may have ended otherwise if Mary Queen of Scots had had her way. The young Catholic Queen endured a series of stormy confrontations at court with the unbending leader of the Scottish Reformation and once charged him with treason. After Knox warned in a sermon in 1563 that Mary's rumored marriage to the son of Spain's monarch, Philip II, would "bring God's vengeance upon the country," she summoned him to answer for his remarks.

Distraught, weeping, and vowing revenge, the queen lashed out: "What have you to do with my marriage, or what are you in this common-wealth?"[92] Knox had warned against the union because it would place on the throne an "infidel" whose father persecuted Protestants. He told the queen that God had set him as a "watchman, both over the realm, and over the kirk [church] of God gathered within the same." For that reason, he said, "I was bound in conscience to blow the trumpet publicly" at any "apparent danger."

John Knox
(American Vision)

If the Scottish nobility consented to the presumed marriage, he told the queen, they would "renounce Christ," "banish His truth from them," and "betray the freedom of the realm."[93] As Dr. D. James Kennedy explained, "Knox knew that God had placed him as a leader in two realms: the realm of faith and the realm of society."[94]

Battle of Lexington *(American Vision)*

"I Have Trained Them for This Very Hour"

Jonas Clark knew it as well. Clark, a 1752 graduate of Harvard, had pastored the church at Lexington for 20 years by the time British Redcoats faced off with his parishioners at Lexington Green on April 19, 1775. The night before the British arrived, Clark met with patriot leaders John Hancock and Samuel Adams at his home. Armed with intelligence that the British were on the march toward Lexington, these two visitors asked Clark if the villagers would fight. "I have trained them for this very hour," Clark said. They would be willing to both fight and die he said, "under the shadow of the house of God."[95]

Indeed, twelve years earlier, some of these men had undoubtedly heard him give a short sermon to his young parishioners, in which he had instructed them about the "important Errand" for which

New England's founders had come into the new world. "It was," he said, "for the sake of God, Religion, Liberty of conscience and the free Enjoyment of the Gospel in its simplicity." Clark was ensuring, as historian Harry Stout states, that "the rising generation would be prepared to take their turn in the long line of worthies who had defined and embodied New England's innermost meaning for over a century."[96] When the militia men who had sat under Pastor Clark's preaching were fired upon by the British, eight died. When he saw the fallen, Clark said, "From this day will be dated the liberty of the world."

Just as Knox, Clark knew that God had placed him as a leader in two realms. He did not fail to address the storm brewing with England. He knew, along with other New England ministers who formed the so-called "Black Regiment" of the Revolutionary era, that his duty was to apply Scripture to every area of life, including politics. These clergymen understood, as Stout states, that "they would be remiss if, as God's watchmen, they failed to sound the alarm."[97]

No Neutral Ground

Knox, Clark, and all those of the Black Regiment who supplied the "moral force which won our independence"[98] understood that they could not remain silent. They responded to the call to become involved. They accepted that there is no morally neutral ground in the entire universe. Every square inch on heaven and earth, as Christian philosopher Cornelius Van Til states, is subject to the contest between Christ and Satan:

No one can stand back, refusing to become involved. He is involved from the day of his birth and even from before his birth. Jesus said: "He that is not with me is against me, and he that gathered not with me scattereth abroad." If you say that you are "not involved," you are, in fact, involved in Satan's side.[99]

Cornelius Van Til
(American Vision)

Esther, the young Jewish woman who became queen in Persia, faced the choice of whether to become involved when her people faced genocide. When she trusted God, He used her to save her entire people from perishing.

In the Parable of the Good Samaritan, a priest and a Levite passed by on the other side, rather than become involved and give aid to a man who had been mugged on the road to Jericho. They not only failed to love their neighbor, they ignored the wounds of a victim of evil. Likewise Christians who today ignore the plight of the unborn and remain indifferent and uninvolved, fail to love their unborn neighbor and wind up aiding evil by their inaction.

Church Free Speech Is the Reason for the First Amendment

Christians have not only a duty, but also the right, as Americans, to prescribe biblical solutions to public moral questions. The whole purpose of the First Amendment, according to American University Professor Daniel Dreisbach, was "to create an environment in which churchmen and moral spokesmen, in general, could speak out boldly without restraint or fear of retribution on matters of public morality."

Dreisbach told a Coral Ridge Ministries conference in 2005 that "the founders wanted the prophetic voice of the church to be free to judge civil society in terms of the Word of God." With their ears still ringing from the clerical moral pronouncements that compelled the colonies to fight, the founders well understood that "the very survival of the civil state . . . is dependent on Christian principles shaping public values and morals, guiding the consciences of its public leaders, and informing public policy and law."

A pastor who speaks out on moral and political concerns, said Dreisbach, is doing "exactly what the First Amendment was written to encourage clergymen to do. That pastor is not threatening the First Amendment; he's living the First Amendment."[100]

Daniel Dreisbach

He is also performing a public service. As Dr. Kennedy stated in testimony presented to members of the U.S. House of Representatives in 2002, "In a culture like ours, which sometimes seems on moral life support, the voice of the church and her message of reconciliation, virtue, and hope must not be silenced."[101]

Sadly, as Francis Schaeffer has pointed out, we Christians have too often been far too silent. In the following chapter, we will see that there may be consequences for such silence; God holds His people accountable for their civic stewardship.

TRUTH 9

God Holds His People Accountable for Their Civic Stewardship

Standing at the towering mahogany pulpit of Coral Ridge Presbyterian Church in 1982, Christian philosopher Francis Schaeffer unleashed a harsh indictment against the church in the West. With his long gray hair, goatee, and compact frame stuffed into a business suit, he both looked and sounded like a modern-day prophet.

One of the most influential Christian thinkers of the twentieth century, Schaeffer outlined how a Judeo-Christian moral consensus has given way in the West to the triumph of secular materialism. Then he asked this question: "Where have the Bible-believing Christians been in the last 40 years?"

Instead of protest and opposition, Schaeffer said, "There has been a vast silence." So much so, that "it was almost like sticking pins into the evangelical constituency in most places to get them interested in the issue of human life." Schaeffer produced a seminar and film series on the sanctity of human life with his son, Frank, and Dr. C. Everett Koop. That effort, *Whatever Happened to the Human Race?*, proved a very hard sell to churches.[102]

Francis Schaeffer

It was the same for noted theologian, author, and teacher R.C. Sproul. Of the some 60 books he has written, the first one to go out of print was *Abortion: A Rational Look at an Emotional Issue*, published in 1990. According to Sproul, churches refused to use the book and its accompanying educational resources for fear that the topic of abortion would divide congregations.[103]

The silence of the church has also been evident at the polls. Less than half of the entire adult population voted in federal elections between 1960 and 2006.[104] Sadly, the turnout rate for self-described Christians is about the same.[105]

Some Say Keep Silent

Cal Thomas
(Handout Photo)

Some voices within the Christian community encourage Christians to keep silent or, at the very least, to pipe down when it comes to civic and cultural concerns. Authors Cal Thomas and Ed Dobson charge in their 1998 book, *Blinded by Might*, that Christian political action has proved futile. In the campaign to end abortion, "twenty years of fighting has won nothing" they say. "And our record," they write, "is no better with other moral and social issues."[106]

Popular Bible teacher John MacArthur has written that "God does not call the church to influence the

Noah Webster
(American Vision)

culture by promoting legislation. . . ."[107] While acknowledging that there is some modest value to political participation, MacArthur believes that "In the truest sense, the moral, social, and political state of a people is irrelevant to the advance of the gospel."[108]

The Founders took a different view. Noah Webster (1758-1843), whom we know for his dictionary, educated five generations of school children with his Blue-backed Speller books. He has been called the "Father of American Scholarship and Education." For Webster, political participation, specifically voting, was a duty owed to God:

> When you become entitled to exercise the right of voting for public officers, let it be impressed on your mind that God commands you to choose for rulers, "just men who will rule in the fear of God." The preservation of government depends on the faithful discharge of this duty; if the

citizens neglect their duty, and place unprincipled men in office, the government will soon be corrupted; laws will be made, not for the public good so much as for selfish or local purposes; corrupt or incompetent men will be appointed to execute the laws; the public revenues will be squandered on unworthy men; and the rights of the citizens will be violated or disregarded. If a republican government fails to secure public prosperity and happiness, it must be because the citizens neglect the divine commands, and elect bad men to make and administer the laws.[109]

Samuel Adams, who has been called the "Father of the American Revolution," thought much the same. He wrote:

Let each citizen remember at the moment he is offering his vote that he is not making a present or a compliment to please an individual —or at least that he ought not so to do; but that he is executing one of the most solemn trusts in human society for which he is accountable to God and his country.[110]

The Founders were steeped in the Scriptures. They knew, as Webster indicates above, of God's requirement that "He who rules over men must be just, ruling in the fear of God" (2 Samuel 23:3). Under Mosaic law, God's people had a civic responsibility to

Samuel Adams
(Library of Congress)

choose their leaders. Moses instructed the Jewish nation to "appoint judges and officers in all your gates, which the Lord your God gives you, according to your tribes, and they shall judge the people with just judgment" (Deuteronomy 16:18).

The people even had a duty to confirm God's choice for a leader. While there was no direct election, Moses told the people, "you shall surely set a king over you whom the Lord your God chooses" (Deuteronomy 17:15).

Liable for Our Leaders

That duty to choose left the people answerable to God for their leaders. "When the citizens have a voice in the selection and direction of their civil leaders," Ken Connor and John Revell, authors of *Sinful Silence*, state, "God holds both the leaders and the citizens accountable for the civil sins of the government." That is why Isaiah aims his accusation over Judah's sins at both rulers and ruled: "Hear the word of the Lord, You *rulers* of Sodom; Give ear to the law of our God, You *people* of Gomorrah" (Isaiah 1:10).

The acts of repentance to which God called Judah were not just personal, but social and political in character. God calls the people not just to "Put away the evil of your doings from before My eyes," but also to "seek justice, rebuke the oppressor, defend the fatherless, plead for the widow" (Isaiah 1:17).

If God held the people of Judah accountable for the actions of their rulers, it seems quite likely that we American Christians, blessed with the freedom to organize, campaign, and vote, will face equal or greater accountability. "When Christians neglect their civil duty," Connor and Revell write, "they need not expect deliverance from the national consequences to follow."[111]

On the other hand, when Christians do the opposite and diligently fulfill not just their duty toward God, but also their civic duty to

Caesar, they set the stage for His blessings on their land. As the Bible states, "When the righteous are in authority, the people rejoice" (Proverbs 29:2), and "Righteousness exalts a nation" (Proverbs 14:34).

Our challenge is to fulfill both of those duties with equal fervency and faithfulness. As Dr. D. James Kennedy has said:

> Salt and light are what Christians are commanded—every one of us—to be. That, I think, is the answer to the problems we face in this country, as individuals, as a nation, and as a world…. We need to proclaim the Gospel, if people's lives are going to be changed, but we need for Christians to get involved in the culture, if we are going to bring that transforming power of Christ to bear on every facet of life.[112]

That two-fold duty to be salt and light in the culture includes both holding our rulers accountable for their actions and exerting the influence of biblical morality on our legislators. Also, as we shall see in the final chapter of this booklet, it includes sharing with our fellow citizens the healing power of God's grace for their lives by introducing them to the incomparable Christ.

TRUTH 10

The Most Political Act Is to Win Someone to Faith in Christ

He was young, smart, wealthy, and the life of every party. Elected to the British Parliament in 1780 at age 21, William Wilberforce was a much-in-demand man about town who delighted and regaled fellow revelers with his wit and sparkling conversation.

He "won his welcome to the luxurious clubs and great private houses," writes biographer John Pollock, "because he was rich, he was amusing, could turn a bon mot and had a keen sense of the ludicrous."[113] A stirring orator, he used his eloquence and incandescent personality to win political office and had no greater aim in life, he later said, than his own fame—what he called "his darling object."

But after this lively young man of promise spent long hours debating Christianity with a traveling companion and former tutor, Isaac Milner, what Wilberforce called his "great change" began to take place. By late 1785, he had embraced evangelical Christianity.

Leave Politics?

His first impulse was to retire from politics—considered by most evangelicals of his day to be worldly and to be avoided.[114] But a conversation with John Newton, the former slave ship captain turned minister, who is best known for writing "Amazing Grace," helped change his mind. He told the young man not to leave politics. As Newton later put it in a letter to Wilberforce, "It is hoped

William Wilberforce
(American Vision)

and believed that the Lord has raised you up for the good of His church and for the good of the nation."[115]

Wilberforce soon reached the conclusion that God had indeed called him to pursue two great goals: the abolition of the slave trade and the reformation of the low state of British morals. He set after his twin ambitions with enormous energy. By the end of his life, his goals had largely been achieved. His persistent call to end the British slave trade finally won approval in Parliament in 1807, and in 1833, only three days before his death, the House of Commons abolished slavery throughout the British Empire, bringing freedom to some 800,000 slaves.[116]

The impact Wilberforce made on Britain's moral climate was almost equally great. "It is a matter of history," states his biographer, "that for two generations, at least, after Wilberforce, the British character was molded by attitudes that were essentially his. Under his

C. S. Lewis
*(Used by permission of The Marion
E. Wade Center, Wheaton College)*

leadership, a Christian social conscience attacked prevalent social ills while at the same time seeking to better the lives of those affected by them."[117]

Isaac Milner could not have known what he had set in motion while discussing Christianity with Wilberforce on their way to the French-Italian Riviera. His willingness to present the case for Christianity impacted not just one life, but millions. As C. S. Lewis once said, "He who converts his neighbour has performed the most practical Christian-political act of all."[118]

One Conversion Can Shake a Nation

Wilberforce does not stand alone, however, as an example of how conversion can bring political change. Philippines dictator Ferdinand Marcos threw rival politician Benigno Aquino into prison in 1972. There he met Christ, after reading the story of Charles Colson's conversion in his book, *Born Again*.

Aquino, a darling of the people, had first been elected to office at age 22. He was later exiled to the United States, but decided to return in 1983 to lead a peaceful resistance to the corrupt Marcos regime. When his plane touched down in Manila, soldiers arrived to take him off the plane, and within seconds he was dead.

The impact of his life did not end with his death. Aquino's political assassination, mourned by two million people who walked in the rain to his funeral, set in motion not a bloody revolution, but the famed "people power" uprising that led to Marcos' ouster and the introduction of democratic government in the Philippines.[119]

"One can never quite calculate how one conversion like Benigno Aquino's in a lowly prison cell," Colson writes, "may set in motion a train of events to shake a nation."[120]

As a co-founder of the Moral Majority, Dr. D. James Kennedy was a passionate advocate for Christian civic involvement to "reclaim America for Christ." He was also the founder of the world's most-used method for telling others about Christ. He understood that evangelism can achieve what politics *alone* cannot. "We Christians will never impose biblical morality on a predominantly non-Christian culture," he wrote. "It will not happen. They will rise up and throw it off." It is only when Christians "share the Gospel with others that individual lives—and ultimately, cultures—are transformed by the power of Christ and His Word."[121]

Saving Souls Saves the Nation

Nineteenth century American evangelicals understood the link between the gospel and politics. A Library of Congress exhibit, "Religion and the Founding of the American Republic" reports that "converting their fellow citizens to Christianity was, for them, an act that simultaneously saved souls and saved the republic." The American Home Missionary Society told supporters in 1826 that "we are doing the work of patriotism no less than Christianity."[122]

Voting, lobbying, volunteering for political campaigns, even running for office, are all important. They are all part of our duty to Caesar, but they cannot take the place of our duty to God—to bring Christ's message of forgiveness and freedom from sin to those whom we meet every day. When we do that, the gospel will work its way into every area and yield enormous dividends, eternal and temporal, in both private and public life.

As was stated in the Introduction, we cannot wait for a new generation of leaders to rise up and lead us. Each of us must take responsibility for carrying out our own Christian civic duty in the arena of government and politics. Each of us is responsible to daily share with others the wonderful message of Christ's deliverance from sins. Our prayer is that this little booklet has helped you understand more clearly how you can enter the arena, for "He who is in you is greater than he who is in the world" (I John 4:4b).

ENDNOTES

Introduction

1   Billy Graham, "A Time for Moral Courage," *Reader's Digest*, July 1962, 49. Quoted in Tom Minnery, *Why You Can't Stay Silent* (Wheaton, Illinois: Tyndale House Publishers, 2001), 51.

2   Ibid., 51. Quoted in Minnery, 51.

3   Jeffrey K. Hadden and Charles E. Swann, *Prime Time Preachers: The Rising Power of Televangelism* (Reading, Massachusetts: Addison-Wesley, 1981), 60. Quoted in Richard John Neuhaus, *The Naked Public Square: Religion and Democracy in America* (Grand Rapids: Eerdmans, 1984), 10.

4   "Memorial Service Honors, Remembers, D. James Kennedy," *Impact* [newsletter of Coral Ridge Ministries], October 2007, 3.

Truth 1: The Foundation of Government and Politics Is Religion

5   *Everson v. Board of Education*, 330 U.S. 1 (1947). The Court in this case both established a radical separation of church and state and, ironically, upheld a school board policy in which parents who sent their children to Catholic schools were reimbursed for the cost of public bus transportation.

6   Will and Ariel Durant, *The Lessons of History* (New York: Simon and Schuster, 1968), 50. Quoted in Charles Colson, *Kingdoms in Conflict* (William Morrow/Zondervan, 1987), 229.

7   David Aikman, *Jesus in Beijing* (Washington, D.C.: Regnery Publishing, 2003), 5.

8   Charles Francis Adams, editor, *The Works of John Adams, Second President of the United States*, (Boston: Little, Brown & Company, 1854), 229.

9   Estimates for the death toll during the French Revolution's "Reign of Terror" vary. A compilation of sources, "Statistics of Wars, Oppressions and Atrocities of the Eighteenth Century," presents a range from different scholarly sources of 27,000 to 263,000. See http://users.erols.com/mwhite28/wars18c.htm#FrRev1, accessed 2/22/08.

10   Francis Schaeffer, *A Christian Manifesto* (Wheaton, ILL.: Crossway Books, 1981), 45.

11   Paul Kengor, *God and Ronald Reagan* (New York: HarperCollins, 2004), 146.

12   "Abortion in the United States: Statistics and Trends," National Right to Life Committee, Accessed 2/22/08 at http://www.nrlc.org/abortion/facts/abortionstats.html.

13   Barry Lynn, *Piety and Politics*, (New York: Harmony Books, 2006),10.

14   Richard John Neuhaus, *The Naked Public Square: Religion and Democracy in America* (Grand Rapids: Eerdmans Publishing Co., 1984), 28.

Truth 2: Christianity Makes the Best Foundation for Law And Politics.

15   David Cherry, editor, *The Roman World: A Sourcebook* (Malden, Mass.: Blackwell Publishers, 2001), 51.

16   W. E. H. Lecky, *History of European Morals: From Augustus to Charlemagne*, vol. 2 (New York: Vanguard Press, 1927), 24. Quoted in Alvin J. Schmidt, *How Christianity Changed the World* (Grand Rapids, Michigan: Zondervan 2004), 51.

17   Schmidt, 52.

18   Rodney Stark, *The Rise of Christianity: A Sociologist Reconsiders History* (Princeton, New Jersey: Princeton University Press, 1996), 118.

19   George Grant, *The Third Time Around: A History of the Pro-Life Movement from the First Century to the Present* (Brentwood, Tennessee: Wolgemuth & Hyatt, 1991), 20.

20   Schmidt, 51.

21   Ibid., 51.

22   Tom Minnery, *Why You Can't Stay Silent* (Wheaton, Illinois: Tyndale House Publishers, 2001), 20.

23   Gary DeMar, *You've Heard It Said: 15 Biblical Misinterpretations That Render Christians Powerless* (Brentwood, Tennessee: Wolgemuth & Hyatt, 1991), 78.

24   Minnery, 22.

25   D. James Kennedy and Jerry Newcombe, *What if the Bible Had Never Been Written?* (Nashville, Tennessee: Thomas Nelson, 1998), 49.

26   Kennedy and Newcombe, 49.

27   Schmidt, 56, 57.

28   Schmidt, 268.

29   Peter Hammond, "King Alfred the Great," *Christian Action for Reformation and Revival,* Vol 1(2008): 12-13.

30   J. M. Roberts, *History of the World* (New York: Oxford University Press, 1993), 243-244. Kennedy and Newcombe, 51.

31   Henry Mayr-Harting, "The West: The Age of Conversion (700-1050)," in John McManners, ed. *The Oxford Illustrated History of Christianity* (New York: Oxford University Press, 1990), 101. Quoted in DeMar, *You've Heard It Said*, 111.

32   Hammond, 12-13.

33   Richard L. Perry, editor, *Sources of Our Liberties* (Chicago: American Bar Foundation, 1978), 1.

34   Kennedy and Newcombe, 53.

Truth 3: The Bible Gives Guidance for Governments and Citizens

35   Gary DeMar, *Ruler of the Nations* (Powder Springs, Georgia: American Vision 2001), 115.

36   Merrill C. Tenney, *New Testament Times* (Grand Rapids, Michigan: Eerdmans, 1965), 152. Quoted in Gary DeMar, *You've Heard It Said* (Brentwood, Tennessee: Wolgemuth & Hyatt, 1991), 68.

37   Charles Colson, *Kingdoms in Conflict* (William Morrow/Zondervan, 1987), 114.

Truth 4: Without God, Government Is a Fearful Master

38   "Humanist Manifesto," Accessed 2/22/2008 at American Humanist Association website: http://www.americanhumanist.org/about/manifesto1.html.

39   "Genocide in the 20th Century: Stalin's Forced Famine, 1932-1933, 7,000,000 Deaths," The History Place website. Accessed 2/23/2008 at http://www.historyplace.com/worldhistory/genocide/stalin.htm.

40   Rudolph J. Rummel, *Lethal Politics: Soviet Genocide and Mass Murder Since 1917* (New Brunswick, New Jersey: Transaction Publishers, 1990), 296.

41   Rummel, 12.

42   Robert Conquest, *The Great Terror: A Reassessment* (New York: Oxford University Press, 1990), 252.

43   James F. Pontuso, *Assault on Ideology: Aleksandr Solzhenitsyn's Political Thought* (Lanham, Maryland: Lexington Books, 2004), 10.

44   Aleksandr Solzhenitsyn, *The Gulag Archipelago*, vol. 2 (Boulder, Colorado: Westview Press, 1998), 293.

45   Ron Rosenbaum, *Explaining Hitler: The Search for the Origins of His Evil* (New York: Harper Perennial, 1999), 175.

46   J.S. Conway, *The Nazi Persecution of the Churches, 1933-1945* (Vancouver, BC: Regent College Publishing, 2001), 76.

47   The "Humanist Manifesto I" states, in part, the following: FIRST: Religious humanists regard the universe as self-existing and not created. . . . SECOND: Humanism believes that man is a part of nature and that he has emerged as a result of a continuous process. . . . FIFTH: Humanism asserts that the nature of the universe depicted by modern science makes unacceptable any supernatural or cosmic guarantees of human values. Humanist Manifesto I.

48   George Victor, *Hitler: The Pathology of Evil* (Dulles, Virginia: 2000), 1.

49   Dmitri Volkogonov, *Autopsy for an Empire: The Seven Leaders Who Built the Soviet Regime* (Free Press, 1998), 139.

50   Fyodor Dostoevsky, *The Brothers Karamazov*, trans., Andrew H. MacAndrew (Toronto: Bantam Books, 1970), 760. Quoted in D. James Kennedy, Ph.D., and Jerry Newcombe, *The Presence of a Hidden God* (Colorado Springs, Colorado: Multnomah Books, 2008), 36.

51   James Madison, The Federalist No. 51. Accessed 2/23/2008 at http://www.constitution.org/fed/federa51.htm.

Truth 5: America Was Built by Biblically Literate Citizens

52   David Barton, *Benjamin Rush: Signer of the Declaration of Independence* (Aledo, Texas: WallBuilders, 1999), 8.

53   Barton, back cover.

54   Barton, 34.

55   John Sanderson, *Biography of the Signers to the Declaration of Independence*, Vol. IV (Philadelphia: R.W. Pomeroy, 1823), 281. Quoted in Barton, 99.

56   David Barton, "God: Missing in Action From American History" Online article accessed 2/23/2008 at http://www.wallbuilders.com/LIBissuesArticles.asp?id=100.

57   Alexis de Tocqueville, *Democracy in America*, vol. 2, trans. Henry Reeve; Rev. Francis Bower; ed. Phillips Bradley (New York: Vintage Books, 1958), 6. Quoted in Dr. David C. Gibbs, Jr., *One Nation Under God* (Seminole, Florida: Christian Law Association, 2005), 12.

58   Daniel Webster, *The Great Speeches and Orations of Daniel Webster* (Boston: Little, Brown and Co., 1879), 51.

59   Harry S. Stout, *The New England Soul* (New York: Oxford University Press, 1986), 3.

60   Stout, 4.

61   David W. Hall, editor, *Election Day Sermons* (Oak Ridge, Tennessee: Covenant Foundation, 1996), 22.

62   D. James Kennedy and Jerry Newcombe, *What If Jesus Had Never Been Born?* (Nashville: Thomas Nelson, 1994), 60.

63   David Barton, *A Spiritual Heritage Tour of the United States Capitol* (Aledo, Texas: WallBuilders, 2000), 15.

64   Ibid., 13.

65   Marshall Foster, "Introduction to the 1599 Geneva Bible," Article accessed 2/23/2008 at http://www.tollelegepress.com/gb/geneva_introduction.php.

Truth 6: All Governments Legislate Morality

66   Jesse Ventura, *Do I Stand Alone?: Going to the Mat Against Political Pawns and Media Jackals* (New York: Pocket Books, 2001), 148.

67   "James Buchanan" in *Encyclopedia Americana* by Philip S. Klein. Accessed 2/23/2008 at http://ap.grolier.com/article?assetid=0064690-00.

68   Reclaiming the Culture, 27.

69   "The Challenge of Peace: God's Promise and Our Response, Part 1," U.S. Catholic Bishops. Accessed 2/23/2008 at http://www.osjspm.org/the_challenge_of_peace_1.aspx.

70   Henry Hyde, *For Every Idle Silence* (Ann Arbor, Michigan: Servant Publications, 1985), 36-37.

71   Hyde, 31.

72   Hyde, 12.

73   Hyde, 13.

74   "King Moves North," *Time*, April 30, 1965, Accessed 2/9/08 at http://www.time.com/time/magazine/article/0,9171,898653-1,00.html.

75   Dr. Norman Geisler and Frank Turek, *Legislating Morality* (Minneapolis, Minnesota: Bethany House Publishers, 1998), 37.

76   "The Index Of Leading Cultural Indicators, 2001" Article accessed on 2/9/08 at http://www.valuemovies.net/Parentsvirtues.htm.

Truth 7: Retreat or Rule: Neither Is an Option

77   DeMar, *Ruler of the Nations*, 137.

78   Benjamin Hart, *Faith and Freedom: The Christian Roots of Liberty* (San Bernardino, California: Here's Life Publishers, 1988), 40.

79   Alvin J. Schmidt, *How Christianity Changed the World* (Grand Rapids, Michigan: Zondervan 2004), 261.

80   Charles Colson, *Kingdoms in Conflict* (William Morrow/Zondervan, 1987), 111.

81   Schmidt 261.

82   Gary Amos and Richard Gardiner, *Never Before in History: America's Inspired History* (Dallas, Texas: Haughton Publishing Company, 1998), 8.

83   Colson, 113.

84   Jeffrey K. Hadden and Charles E. Swann, *Prime Time Preachers: The Rising Power of Televangelism* (Reading, Massachusetts: Addison-Wesley, 1981), 60. Quoted in Neuhaus, 10.

85   Francis Schaeffer, *A Christian Manifesto* (Wheaton, IL: Crossway Books, 1981), 18-19.

86   D. James Kennedy, "The Danger of Doing It Alone" Message given June 6, 2002 (Fort Lauderdale, Florida: Coral Ridge Ministries).

87   Schaeffer, 18.

88   Reclaiming the Culture, 23.

89   Conway, 335.

90   Ibid., 78.

91   D. James Kennedy, "The Christian View of Politics," Sermon preached June 1, 1975. (Fort Lauderdale, Florida: Coral Ridge Ministries).

Truth 8: Christians Have the Right and Duty to Speak Biblical Truth to Temporal Power

92   John Knox, *The History of the Reformation of Religion in Scotland* (Glasgow, Scotland: Blackie & Son, 1841), 290.

93   Knox, 290-291. Accessed online.

94   D. James Kennedy, "Is Your Vision God-Sized?" *Impact* (newsletter of Coral Ridge Ministries), May 2001. Accessed 2/23/2008 at http://www.coralridge.org/impact/2001_May_Pg7.htm.

95   "Jonas Clark," *The Encyclopedia Britannica*, vol. 2, (New York: The Werner Company, 1898), 818. Accessed online.

96   Stout, 254, 255.

97   Stout, 284.

98   John Wingate Thornton, *The Pulpit of the American Revolution* (Boston: Gould and Lincoln, 1860), xxxviii. Accessed online.

99   Gary DeMar, *You've Heard It Said* (Brentwood, Tennessee: Wolgemuth & Hyatt, 1991), 53.

100   "First Amendment for Churches," *Impact* (Coral Ridge Ministries newsletter), April 2005, 3. Accessed online 2/23/2008 at http://www.coralridge.org/imp/impact04057.aspx.

101   Statement of D. James Kennedy, Ph.D., President, Coral Ridge Ministries, Fort Lauderdale, Florida.

Testimony Before the Subcommittee on Oversight of the House Committee on Ways and Means Hearing on Review of Internal Revenue Code Section 501 (c)(3) Requirements for Religious Organizations. May 14, 2002. Accessed 2/23/2008 at http://waysandmeans.house.gov/Legacy/oversite/107cong/5-14-02/5-14kenn.htm.

Truth 9: God Holds His People Accountable for Their Civic Stewardship

102   Francis Schaeffer, "A Christian Manifesto," transcript of 1982 presentation at Coral Ridge Presbyterian Church (Fort Lauderdale, Florida: Coral Ridge Ministries), 9.

103   R. C. Sproul, "Entering the Kingdom," *Renewing Your Mind with R.C. Sproul* radio program aired 1/26/08. Accessed online 2/23/08 at http://www.ligonier.org/rym.php.

104   "National Voter Turnout in Federal Elections: 1960–2006," Accessed online 2/23/2008 at http://www.infoplease.com/ipa/A0781453.html.

105   William Bennett, "Executive Summary," *The Index of Leading Cultural Indicators 2001*, Empower.org. Cited in Ken Connor and John Revell, *Sinful Silence: When Christians Neglect Their Civil Duty* (Nashville, Tennessee: Ginosko Publishing, 2004), 45.

106   Cal Thomas and Ed Dobson, *Blinded by Might* (Grand Rapids: Zondervan, 1999), 24.

107   John MacArthur, "Christian Duty in a Pagan Culture," accessed on 2/20/08 at http://www.gty.org/Resources/Articles/2395.

108   John MacArthur, "Christians and Politics (Part 3)" *Pulpit Magazine*, October 19th, 2006. Accessed 2/23/2006 at http://www.sfpulpit.com/2006/10/19/christians-and-politics-part-3/.

109   Noah Webster, *History of the United States* (New Haven: Durrie & Peck, 1832), pp. 307-308.

110   Samuel Adams, *The Writings of Samuel Adams*, Harry Alonzo Cushing, editor (New York: G.P. Putnam's Sons, 1907), Vol. IV, p. 256, in the Boston Gazette on April 16, 1781. Cited at WallBuilders website at http://www.wallbuilders.com/LIBissuesArticles.asp?id=80.

111   Connor and Revell, 26.

112   Dr. D. James Kennedy, "The Danger of Doing It Alone," Message delivered to Coral Ridge Ministries Employee Breakfast, June 6, 2002:(Fort Lauderdale, Florida: Coral Ridge Ministries).

Truth 10: The Most Political Act Is to Win Someone to Faith in Christ.

113   John Pollock, *Wilberforce* (England: Lion Publishing, 1977), 15.

114   Ibid., 39.

115   Ibid., 38.

116   Kevin Belmonte, *William Wilberforce* (Grand Rapids: Zondervan, 2002), 332.

117   John Pollock, "The Little Abolitionist, William Wilberforce," *Christianity Today*, April 21, 1978: 23.

118   C.S. Lewis, *God in the Dock, Essays on Theology and Ethics*. Edited by Walter Hooper. (Grand Rapids, Mich.: Eerdmans, 1970), 199. Quoted in *The Quotable Lewis*, Wayne Martindale, Jerry Lewis, Editors (Wheaton, Illinois: Tyndale House, 1990), 479.

119   Charles Colson, *Kingdoms in Conflict* (William Morrow/Zondervan, 1987), 313-332.

120   Ibid., 315.

121   John Barber, *America Restored* (Fort Lauderdale, Florida: Coral Ridge Ministries, 2002), 5.

122   "Religion and the New Republic," Religion and the Founding of the American Republic, Library of Congress exhibition., Accessed online on 02-17-08 at http://www.loc.gov/exhibits/religion/rel07.html

▶ TAKE THE NEXT STEP!

Video, Website to Help You Learn More!

Once you've read *Ten Truths About Christians and Politics*, ask for the video, *Pastors, Pulpits, and Politics: Christian Rules of Engagement*, featuring Gary DeMar, Mat Staver, Tony Perkins, and Jordan Lorence. This in-depth DVD offers presentations from these Christian leaders on what God, the Constitution, and the IRS say about Christian civic engagement. To request *Pastors, Pulpits, and Politics*, please call 1-800-988-7884 or go to www.coralridge.org.

Website Resources

Plus, please visit the Ten Truths About Christians and Politics section on our website at www.coralridge.org. Just click on the "Equip and Grow" tab and you'll find more resources, including the online text of this booklet, a downloadable PowerPoint presentation, and a handy one-page Ten Truths About Christians and Politics Talking Points.